BACKYARD BIRDS

WOODPECKERS

by Anastasia Suen

crest

bugs

Look for these words and pictures as you read.

beak

chicks

Peck! Peck!
Have you seen this bird?
It is a woodpecker.

crest

This bird has a red crest.
Dads have red on their face, too.
Moms have black and white faces.

bugs

This bird eats bugs.
It pecks to find them.

beak

A sharp beak cuts a hole.
It sounds like a drum.

Mom and Dad make a nest.
They build it in the tree.
They feed the chicks.

A feeder hangs from a tree.
Woodpeckers eat a cake inside.
It is made with fat and seeds.

A woodpecker is a backyard bird. Have you seen it?

crest

bugs

Did you find?

beak

chicks

Spot is published by Amicus Learning, an imprint of Amicus
P.O. Box 227, Mankato, MN 56002
www.amicuspublishing.us

Library of Congress Cataloging-in-Publication Data
Names: Suen, Anastasia author
Title: Woodpeckers / by Anastasia Suen.
Description: Mankato, MN : Amicus Learning, [2026] | Series: Spot backyard birds | Audience: Ages 4–7 | Audience: Grades K–1 | Summary: "Woodpeckers are red, white, and black birds that peck for bugs in the trees. These birds can be found across North America. This search-and-find book reinforces new vocabulary words with simple facts and compelling photographs to teach kindergarten and first grade readers about backyard birds"— Provided by publisher.
Identifiers: LCCN 2025010582 (print) | LCCN 2025010583 (ebook) | ISBN 9798892008341 library binding | ISBN 9798892009003 paperback | ISBN 9798892009669 ebook
Subjects: LCSH: Woodpeckers—Juvenile literature
Classification: LCC QL696.P56 S84 2026 (print) | LCC QL696.P56 (ebook) | DDC 598.7/2–dc23/eng/20250626
LC record available at https://lccn.loc.gov/2025010582
LC ebook record available at https://lccn.loc.gov/2025010583

Ana Brauer, editor
Deb Miner, series designer
Sara Hood, book designer and photo researcher

Photos by Getty Images/Carlos Carreno, 3, GibsonPictures, 2, 4–5, 15, Tempau, 2, 8–9, 15; Shutterstock/Agnieszka Bacal, 1, Connell Fine Art Studio, cover, 16, Harry Collins Photography, 2, 10, 15, hmdavis, 12–13, jamie piccolo, 14, RLS Photo, 2, 6–7, 15